21 DAYS TO LAW OF ATTR-ACTION

21 DAYS to LAW of attr-ACTION

DEEDEE SWANSON

PALMETTO
PUBLISHING
Charleston, SC
www.PalmettoPublishing.com

Copyright © 2024 by DeeDee Swanson

All rights reserved

No portion of this book may be reproduced, stored in a retrieval system, or transmitted in any form by any means—electronic, mechanical, photocopy, recording, or other—except for brief quotations in printed reviews, without prior permission of the author.

Hardcover ISBN: 979-8-8229-5730-5
Paperback ISBN: 979-8-8229-4895-2
eBook ISBN: 979-8-8229-4896-9

Contents

Forward	vii
Need to Know	ix
My Story	xiii
Chapter 1: Self-Talk	1
Chapter 2: Gratitude	5
Chapter 3: Liberation	8
Chapter 4: Rise	12
Chapter 5: Movement	15
Chapter 6: Meditation	17
Chapter 7: Dharma	24
Chapter 8: Goals	27
Chapter 9: Un-fear	30
Chapter 10: Change	32
Chapter 11: ACTION	35
About the Author	39

Forward

The concept behind the Law of Attr-ACTION is centered on the idea that similar energies attract one another, indicating that optimistic or pessimistic thoughts precipitate corresponding experiences in an individual's life. By concentrating on positive thoughts, the likelihood of drawing positive outcomes and prospects increases.

Nonetheless, the synergistic effect of positive thoughts and corresponding actions can significantly enhance the impacts of the Law of Attr-ACTION. Engaging in actions that resonate with positive thoughts can magnify the energy emitted into the universe, thereby boosting the chances of materializing one's desires and aspirations.

In essence, although positive thoughts possess substantial efficacy independently, coupling them with positive behaviors and actions can escalate and expedite the process of manifestation. This combination of mindset and actions serves as a driving force toward attaining one's aspirations and shaping the desired life.

Witnessing the movie "The Secret," my sister, Alisa Swanson, fearlessly resolved to manifest her ideal life partner at the age of 50. Despite my skepticism, given her single status, she succeeded in attracting her dream man, Tony Lazzerini. He embodied everything she sought, free of any past baggage or children. Together, they now relish a splendid life, journeying the globe and living out her envisioned life alongside this extraordinary individual.

To my son, Blake

Need to Know

Law of Attraction: The belief that positive or negative thoughts bring about positive or negative experiences in a person's life by attracting similar energies.

Manifesting: The practice of bringing thoughts and desires into reality by focusing on them with intention and belief.

Dharma: A person's ultimate purpose or calling in life, often associated with fulfilling one's unique destiny or true self.

Visualizing: The technique of creating mental images of desired outcomes or goals to aid in manifesting and attracting them into reality.

Goal Setting: The process of consciously establishing specific goals, intentions, or expectations for desired outcomes.

Self-Talk: The internal dialogue or thoughts that individuals have with themselves, which can greatly influence mindset, beliefs, and ultimately, outcomes in life.

Step-by-step instructions for the "21 Days to Law of Attr-ACTION" journey:

1. Read the book: Start by reading the book completely from beginning to end to familiarize yourself with the content and concepts presented.

2. Habit journey: After reading the book through completely one time, go back to the beginning and start your habit journey. Spend a minimum of twenty-one days practicing each new behavior outlined in the eleven chapters of the book. 21 days per chapter. Read the chapter you are currently working on every morning when you rise and every evening just before going to bed.

3. Bracelet method: As you practice each new behavior, put on a bracelet and keep it on the same wrist throughout the twenty-one-day period for that chapter.

4. Accountability: If you catch yourself reverting to the negative behavior instead of the new habit during the twenty-one days, snap the bracelet against your skin and then switch it to the other wrist and restart that specific chapter and rebegin practicing the new habit again from day one. This is the perfect time to find an accountability partner, this is someone who will hold you accountable to your commitments and goals. This is someone you will text or call everyday to share your personal goals and challenges.

5. Consistency: Remember, it takes twenty-one consistent days to form a new habit, so commit to practicing the new behaviors diligently each day.

6. Unreasonableness: Embrace being unreasonable in your pursuit of positive change and growth throughout the journey.

7. Duration: You have the flexibility to complete the journey in as little as 231 days or take longer as needed. However, the sooner you complete it, the sooner you will see positive changes in your life.

8. End goal: Keep in mind that the goal of this journey is to help your life come together and align with the principles of the Law of Attr-ACTION. Reread the chapter you are working on as often as necessary to keep your focus on that particular habit.

9. Follow these steps diligently, stay committed to the process, and watch as your life transforms positively through the "21 Days to Law of Attr-ACTION" journey.

10. I have included a downloadable work book to assist you as you journey through the chapters. Please see QR code.

21 Days to
Laws of Attr-ACTION

Scan for workbook

My Story

In March 2020, my beloved mother succumbed to congestive heart failure after valiantly battling the illness for eighteen years. She was a pillar of strength and resilience. Amid the backdrop of the COVID-19 pandemic and the collapse of my second marriage, my struggles with alcohol worsened, while depression crept into my life. However, I found solace and support in my sisters, Alisa Lazzerini and Darlene Paulson. I also relied heavily on our lifelong family friend Ben Bufkin and my two dear nieces, Taryn and Vanessa Paulson. Their unwavering presence, alongside the light of my life, my son Blake Thorne and my business, guided me through the darkest moments.

I was fortunate to have a steadfast friend and business partner, Sharon Meyer, who provided immense support during these challenging times, including the closure of one of our day spas due to the pandemic. Overwhelmed by grief from my mother's passing, I reached rock bottom. By 2021, I realized that this was not the life I was destined to lead. Taking decisive action, I initiated a divorce and embarked on a journey of sobriety.

With a renewed determination to shape my own destiny, I embraced the principles of the Law of Attr-ACTION. Soon, my life began to pivot in unexpected ways. Venturing into real estate and investing—my true passions—I left my hometown, sold our day spa of twenty-three years, and settled in a high-rise penthouse in Las Vegas. Sharon and I collaborated to transition from the spa industry to real estate, aligning with my envisioned future.

The transformative journey illuminated in this narrative underscores the power of action in harnessing the Law of Attr-ACTION. Today, I am filled with profound happiness, buoyed by the success of my son as a project manager and real estate licensee. As I envision partnering with my son Blake and his girlfriend Jenna, in the field of investing and real estate, I embrace the exciting prospects of my forthcoming journey with fervor and optimism. By continuing to follow these steps I have laid out for you in this book, I will continue my growth journey, one day at a time, and I hope you will join me.

Everywhere you go, there you are!

Chapter 1
SELF-TALK

A man is but the product of his thoughts. What he thinks he becomes. - **Gandhi**

In our daily lives, the conversations we have with ourselves play a significant role in shaping our thoughts, emotions, and actions. This inner dialogue, often referred to as self-talk, can either be a powerful force that propels us forward or a limiting belief that holds us back. Understanding the importance of positive self-talk and learning how to cultivate it is essential for personal growth and well-being.

The words we choose to say to ourselves can influence our mood, behavior, and perception of the world around us. Negative self-talk can create self-doubt and anxiety and limit our potential. On the other hand, positive self-talk can boost confidence, increase resilience, and foster a more optimistic outlook on life. By being mindful of our internal dialogue, we can actively shape our mindset and attitude toward ourselves and others.

The first step in cultivating positive self-talk is becoming aware of the thoughts running through our minds. Pay attention to the language you use when speaking to yourself. Are you kind and encouraging, or critical and self-sabotaging?

When you catch yourself engaging in negative self-talk, challenge those thoughts. Ask yourself whether there is evidence to support these beliefs or whether there is an alternative, more compassionate way to view the situation (a great book on this subject is "Meditations for Breaking the Habit of Being Yourself" by Joe Dispenza).

Incorporating gratitude into your self-talk can shift your focus toward the positives in your life. Acknowledging your strengths, accomplishments, and blessings and feeling grateful for them can help cultivate a more positive mindset.

Using affirmations is a powerful tool for fostering positive self-talk. Repeat empowering statements such as "I am capable," "I am deserving of love," or "I can overcome challenges" to reinforce a positive self-image. Guided meditations for this can be found on YouTube and are easy to follow.

Visualizing success and positive outcomes can help reframe your self-talk toward a more optimistic perspective. Envision yourself achieving your goals and embodying a sense of confidence and resilience.

Examples of Positive Self-Talk

Instead of saying, "I'm not good enough," try saying, "I am constantly improving and growing in my abilities."

Instead of saying, "I can't do this," try saying, "I may face challenges, but I have the skills and determination to overcome them."

Instead of saying, "I always mess things up," try saying, "I am human, and mistakes are opportunities for learning and growth."

The Ripple Effect of Positive Self-Talk

Embracing positive self-talk is not only beneficial for our individual well-being but also has a ripple effect on our relationships, performance, and overall quality of life. When we cultivate self-compassion, self-confidence, and self-belief through our internal dialogue, we naturally radiate these qualities outward, influencing how we interact with others and how we approach challenges.

By harnessing the power of positive self-talk, we unlock our full potential, cultivate resilience in the face of adversity, and nurture a deep sense of self-acceptance and empowerment. Remember, the way we speak to ourselves matters—choose words that uplift, inspire, and propel you toward a brighter, more fulfilling future.

Reprogramming your subconscious mind without engaging in negative self-talk involves embracing positive encouragement and affirmations. By focusing on uplifting and empowering thoughts, you can gradually shift your mindset toward a more optimistic outlook. Choose affirmations that resonate with you and that reflect the goals and values you wish to embody. Repeat these affirmations daily, visualizing yourself achieving success and embodying the traits you desire. Celebrate your progress and practice self-compassion along the way, recognizing that growth and change take time. With consistent effort and a belief in your ability to transform your subconscious beliefs, you can cultivate a mindset that supports your well-being and success.

Positive self-talk is a powerful tool that can help reprogram your subconscious mind and pave the way for a brighter future. By choosing to fill your internal dialogue with uplifting and empowering words, you are actively shaping your reality in a more positive light. When you consciously replace negative thoughts with affirming ones, you are fostering a mindset of self-belief and confidence. This shift in perspective can have a profound impact on your overall well-being and success, setting the stage for the manifestation of your deepest desires and aspirations. Remember, the words you speak to yourself hold great power, so be kind, be encouraging, and watch as your subconscious mind begins to align with the limitless potential that resides within you.

However, despite these early successes, there came a period during which I strayed off course. This phase underscored to me the vital importance of immersing oneself in a supportive environment filled with positivity and like-minded individuals who also embrace the Law of Attr-ACTION. After all, as the saying goes, like attracts like. If you do not learn to speak positively to yourself, no one else will either, so be kind you deserve it!

Your perception is your reality.

Chapter 2

GRATITUDE

In a world filled with chaos and uncertainty, the practice of gratitude serves as a beacon of light, guiding individuals on a journey toward inner peace and contentment. Gratitude is not merely a fleeting feeling of thankfulness; it is a profound shift in perspective, a way of seeing the world through a lens of appreciation and abundance.

Gratitude has the remarkable ability to transform our lives in ways we never thought possible. When we cultivate a sense of gratitude, we open ourselves up to a multitude of benefits—improved mental health, stronger relationships, increased resilience, and a greater sense of overall well-being.

Research has shown that practicing gratitude regularly can lead to lower levels of stress and anxiety, a boosted immune system, better sleep quality, and increased levels of happiness. By focusing on the positive aspects of our lives and expressing appreciation for the blessings we have, we invite more positivity and abundance into our existence. Gratitude releases the happy hormone.

Gratitude is a practice that requires intention and commitment. It is about actively seeking out moments of joy and goodness in our daily lives, no matter how big or small they may seem. One way to cultivate a grateful heart is to keep a gratitude journal, where we write down things we are thankful for each day. This simple act of reflection can help us shift our focus from what is lacking to what is abundant in our lives.

Another way to cultivate gratitude is through acts of kindness and generosity toward others. When we extend a helping hand or show appreciation to those around us, we not only brighten their day but also deepen our own sense of gratitude and interconnectedness.

Practicing gratitude does not mean ignoring or denying the challenges and hardships we face in life. Rather, it is about acknowledging the difficulties while also recognizing the moments of beauty and grace that coexist alongside them. In times of struggle, gratitude can serve as a lifeline, helping us find strength and resilience in the face of adversity.

By reframing our perspectives and focusing on the lessons we can learn from difficult situations, we can navigate life's challenges with more grace and fortitude. Cultivating gratitude in the midst of hardship is a courageous act that can lead to profound growth and transformation.

As we embrace the practice of gratitude in our lives, we open ourselves up to a world of wonder and abundance. Each moment becomes an opportunity for appreciation, each interaction a chance for connection and kindness. Through gratitude, we come to realize that the greatest gifts are often found in the simplest moments—a smile shared, a sunset observed, a kind word spoken.

So let us embark on this journey of gratitude together, with open hearts and minds, ready to embrace the gift of thankfulness in all its beauty and richness. May we find joy in the ordinary, strength in the difficult, and peace in the chaotic, knowing that gratitude is a guiding light that will always lead us home to ourselves.

Every morning, text your accountability partner ten things that you are grateful for and also text the names of three people you are mentally going to send love to. These three people should have had some negative effect or caused you undue stress regarding their gossip or toxic behavior. Ask your accountability partner to do the same.

The sudden loss of my father Marlin Swanson in 2006 hit me with overwhelming force, as if a ton of bricks had fallen upon me. This divided me from the natural gratitude that I had always practiced innatly. I had always feared and dreaded this moment throughout my life, knowing it would eventually arrive. I was undeniably a daddy's girl, and no one could compare to my father. Overwhelmed with sorrow and despair, I found solace in my second marriage to a man I believed was my ideal partner. However, as I grappled with my grief, I found myself straying further from my path. Seeking refuge in alcohol, I fell into a downward spiral of negativity. As my marriage took its toll on me, I began to realize the toxicity that surrounded me, be careful who you surround yourself with, because that is truly what you become. We did not practice gratitude—huge mistake. I still had so much to be grateful for!

Gratitude can transform common days into thanksgiving, turn routine jobs into joy, and change ordinary opportunities into blessings. - Benjamin Franklin

Chapter 3

LIBERATION

Don't let negative and toxic people rent space in your head. Raise the rent and kick them out. **- Robert Tew**

In a world filled with judgments, opinions, and expectations, it can be easy to get caught up in the whirlwind of what others think or say about you. However, it is essential to understand that your worth and identity are not determined by the perceptions of those around you. True freedom and empowerment come from within, from embracing your authentic self and letting go of the need for external validation. In this chapter, we will explore the art of not caring about what others think or say about you, empowering yourself to rise above negativity and gossip, and reclaiming your sense of self-worth and confidence. This by far is one of the most difficult things to train yourself to do, but by far one of the most rewarding.

Before diving into strategies to detach yourself from the opinions of others, it is crucial to understand the root of these judgments. People's perceptions of you are often influenced by their own beliefs, insecurities, fears, and biases. It is not a reflection of your worth or character but a projection of their own inner world. Recognizing this can help you develop empathy toward those who criticize or gossip about you, understanding that it stems from their own struggles rather than your actions or qualities.

To break free from the shackles of negative opinions, you must shift your mindset toward self-acceptance and self-love. Focus on embracing your strengths, values, and uniqueness, rather than seeking approval from others. Remind yourself that your worth is inherent and does not depend on external validation. Practice positive affirmations, gratitude, and self-care to nurture a strong sense of self-worth that remains unaffected by outside influences.

Developing resilience is key to withstanding criticism and judgment effectively. Embrace challenges as opportunities for growth rather than as validations of your inadequacy. Learn to separate constructive feedback from baseless criticism, and use it to improve yourself without compromising your authenticity. Build confidence in your abilities, values, and decisions, trusting in your intuition and inner guidance above external noise.

Establishing boundaries is essential in protecting your mental and emotional well-being from toxic influences. Surround yourself with supportive, positive individuals who uplift and inspire you, while distancing yourself from those who drain your energy or spread negativity. Prioritize self-care activities that nourish your mind, body, and spirit, helping you stay grounded and resilient in the face of external pressures.

Mindfulness techniques, such as meditation and deep breathing, can help you cultivate inner peace and detachment from external distractions. We will learn more about this in the next few chapters. By focusing on the present moment and observing your thoughts and emotions without judgment, you can develop a sense of inner calm and clarity. Practice letting go of the need for approval or validation, understanding that what others say or think about you is none of your business and does not define your worth.

Ultimately, true empowerment comes from embracing your authentic self and living in alignment with your values and passions.

Release the burden of trying to please everyone or conform to societal expectations, and instead, celebrate your uniqueness and individuality. Remember that you are worthy, capable, and deserving of love and respect, regardless of what others think or say about you. By freeing yourself from the shackles of external opinions, you can step into your power and live a life of authenticity, joy, and freedom.

It's definitely not easy to rise above negativity and gossip! Dealing with situations where people are actively spreading lies and slandering your reputation can be emotionally taxing and challenging to stay positive. The hurtful words and false accusations may feel like a constant weight on your shoulders, making it difficult to move forward and maintain a sense of peace. It's natural to feel angry, betrayed, and frustrated in such circumstances, but it's crucial not to let these negative emotions consume you. They can't hurt you, if you do not allow them in your head!

To prevent individuals from controlling your life with their slander, it's essential to focus on your own truth and integrity. Remind yourself of your values, strengths, and the positive aspects of your life that are separate from their toxic behavior. Surround yourself with supportive friends and family who uplift you and validate your worth. Engaging in activities that bring you joy, practicing self-care, and seeking professional help if needed can also help you maintain a sense of balance and resilience. Furthermore, individuals who are spreading rumors about you, the key to reclaiming your power is not letting their actions dictate your emotions. By not engaging in their drama, responding to their attacks, or seeking revenge, you demonstrate your strength and unwillingness to be dragged down to their level. Remember that your worth is not defined by their words or actions, and taking the high road will ultimately empower you to rise above the negativity and live a more fulfilling and positive life.

In conclusion, reclaiming your sense of self-worth and confidence requires a deep commitment to yourself and a willingness to let go of the need for external validation. By understanding the source of external judgments, reframing your mindset, cultivating resilience and confidence, setting boundaries, practicing mindfulness, and embracing authenticity, you can liberate yourself from the opinions of others and empower yourself to live a life true to your essence. Remember, what people say and think about you is none of your business!

If you don't allow them in your mind, they will not be in your life!

Chapter 4

RISE

Every morning, you have two choices: continue to sleep with your dreams or wake up and chase them. —Arnold Schwarzenegger

The choice to wake up at 4:30 or 5 a.m. daily is a commitment to self-discipline and personal growth. By embarking on this journey, you are setting yourself up for success, productivity, and a head start on the day ahead. The early hours of the morning offer a quiet, undisturbed sanctuary for self-reflection, goal setting, and focused work. Let's explore how embracing the early bird mentality can transform your life in just twenty-one days. Waking up early offers a range of benefits that can positively impact one's day and overall well-being. Starting the day early provides the opportunity for a peaceful and productive start, allowing individuals to have more time to focus on important tasks without the distractions that come later in the day. Early risers often report feeling more energized, proactive, and mentally sharp, which can lead to increased productivity and a greater sense of accomplishment. Additionally, waking up early can also provide time for self-care activities such as exercise, meditation, or enjoying a leisurely breakfast, setting a positive tone for the rest of the day while promoting better physical health and mental wellness. It is imperative to do a ten-minute guided manifestation meditation each morning and every evening. This is the perfect time to text your accountability partner, work on your goals and invisioning them clearly.

If you partake in drinking alcohol or use recreational drugs, I would highly suggest not doing so for the twenty-one days to train yourself to rise early. If this becomes problematic for you, you may need to seek treatment to learn to live a sober life if you want to achieve your ultimate goals and life.

Day 1-7: Planting the Seeds of Discipline

As you begin this twenty-one-day journey, the first week is crucial for establishing a routine and overcoming the initial challenges of rising at your set time no later than 5 a.m. Set a consistent bedtime, create a peaceful evening routine that includes ten minutes of bedtime mediation, and prepare your environment for a smooth morning transition. Start each day with a positive affirmation, reminding yourself of the benefits of early rising and the power of self-discipline.

Day 8-14: Building Momentum and Resilience

During the second week, you may encounter moments of resistance and fatigue as your body adjusts to the new waking time. Stay focused on your goals and the long-term benefits of early rising. Use this time for introspection, journaling, exercise, or pursuing creative endeavors. Embrace the silence of the early morning hours as a time for personal growth and self-care.

Day 15-21: Embracing the Early Bird's Advantage

By the third week, you will notice a remarkable shift in your mindset, energy levels, and productivity. You are now ahead of the curve, gaining valuable time while others are still in slumber. Use this extra time for goal setting, planning your day, exercise, meditation, or engaging in activities that bring you joy. Celebrate your progress and the discipline you have cultivated over the past twenty-one days.

Example of positive self-talk: "I am the master of my mornings and the architect of my success. By rising at 5 a.m. daily, I am maximizing my potential and creating a life of purpose, focus, and fulfillment."

As you complete the twenty-one-day journey to self-discipline and early rising, remember that this practice is not just about waking up early—it is about honoring your commitment to personal growth, productivity, and well-being. Embrace the early bird mentality as a powerful tool for success and continue to cultivate the habit of early rising as a cornerstone of your daily routine. By starting your day at 5 a.m., you are setting yourself apart from the crowd and creating a life of intention, purpose, and excellence.

Learn these new habits & be unrecognizable in eight months!

Chapter 5

MOVEMENT

We see in order to move; we move in order to see —William Gibson

Physical activity plays a crucial role in maintaining optimal health and well-being. Incorporating movement into our daily routines can have a significant effect on our physical, mental, and emotional health. The benefits of regular exercise are abundant, ranging from improved cardiovascular health to enhanced mood and cognitive function. You must commit to this daily!

One of the simplest yet most effective ways to introduce movement into our lives is by committing to at least twenty minutes of physical activity every day. This could be as simple as going for a brisk walk, taking the stairs instead of the elevator, or following a short workout routine. Engaging in physical activity for just twenty minutes a day can bring about a multitude of benefits. It does not need to be done all at once it can be done in five or ten min increments.

First and foremost, regular movement helps to maintain a healthy weight and prevent various chronic conditions such as obesity, heart disease, and diabetes. By burning calories and strengthening our muscles, we can improve our overall physical fitness and reduce the risk of developing these health issues. Strive for 3600 to 10,000 steps everyday.

Furthermore, daily physical activity can have a profound effect on our mental and emotional well-being. Exercise has been shown to reduce stress and anxiety levels, boost mood, and enhance cognitive function. The release of endorphins during physical activity can create a sense of euphoria and well-being, often referred to as the "runner's high." By engaging in daily movement, we can better manage stress and improve our mental health.

If you are already physically active, increasing the duration of your workouts to at least an hour can further amplify these benefits. Longer sessions of exercise allow for greater calorie expenditure, increased muscle strength, and improved cardiovascular endurance. Whether it's through cardiovascular activities such as running or cycling, strength training exercises, or yoga sessions, dedicating more time to physical activity can lead to enhanced physical fitness and overall health.

In conclusion, movement and daily physical activity are essential components of a healthy lifestyle. By committing to just twenty minutes of exercise each day, we can reap the numerous benefits that come with an active lifestyle. If you already prioritize fitness, extending their workouts to at least an hour can provide even greater rewards. Remember, every step, every rep, and every minute of physical activity contributes to a healthier, happier you.

Let's get moving!

Chapter 6

MEDITATION

If you want a new outcome, you will have to break the habit of being yourself, and reinvent a new self —Joe Dispenza

I suggest guided meditations by Jessica Heslop, Jason Stephenson, Joe Dispenza. You will find them on YouTube. Please align the meditation with the daily focus. It is best to meditate first thing in the morning when you awaken and last thing at night before you fall asleep.

For me, from a very young age, I possessed a natural understanding of the Law of Attr-ACTION that seemed to be ingrained within me. The visions of my desired future were crystal clear in my mind, and I wielded a skill in manifesting those dreams with precision. An example of this was when I materialized my dream car at the tender age of sixteen—a sleek black and silver Porsche 914, a vision that had been with me since a family trip to New York when I was just five years old. Acquiring that precise car as my own vehicle at sixteen felt like the realization of a destiny I had long foreseen.

Day 1:
As you embark on this journey of twenty-one days to enforce the habit of ten-minute meditation, take a deep breath in and exhale slowly. Find a quiet and comfortable space where you can relax and focus

your mind. Close your eyes and visualize a bright light surrounding you, filling you with positivity and motivation. Today, let's begin with setting a clear intention for the next twenty-one days: to cultivate a habit of daily ten-minute meditation for manifesting positivity and motivation in our lives. Visualize the life you would like to live and how it will feel once you have accomplished your goals. Its imperative that you are able to experience the actual feelings of your success. How does it feel to live the life of your dreams?

Day 2:
As you sit down for your ten-minute meditation session today, let go of any doubts or distractions. Focus on your breath, feeling the air enter and exit your body. With each inhale, envision yourself breathing in motivation and positivity. With each exhale, release any negative thoughts or self-limiting beliefs. Visualize your goals and dreams coming to fruition, filling you with a sense of excitement and purpose.

Day 3:
It's the third day of your twenty-one-day journey toward manifesting motivation through meditation. Today, reflect on the power of consistency and commitment. By dedicating just ten minutes of your day to this practice, you are creating a positive shift in your mindset and energy. Embrace the feelings of gratitude and abundance as you meditate, knowing that you have the power to manifest your desires through focused intention and action.

Day 4:
As you meditate today, focus on the present moment. Let go of worries about the future or regrets from the past. Stay grounded in the now, appreciating the blessings that surround you. Feel the energy within you growing stronger with each breath, fueling your motivation and determination. Trust in the process and believe in your ability to create the life you desire through consistent practice and positive thinking.

Day 5:
Today you need commitment to the process. Celebrate each day of dedicated practice as a step toward building a habit that will transform your life. Embrace any challenges or distractions that arise, knowing that you have the strength and resilience to overcome them. Stay connected to your motivations and intentions, allowing them to guide you toward success.

Day 6:
As you meditate today, visualize yourself stepping into your highest potential. See yourself achieving your goals, living a life filled with joy, abundance, and fulfillment. Let this vision ignite a fire of motivation within you, inspiring you to take action toward manifesting your dreams. Through daily practice and unwavering belief in your abilities, you are creating a reality that aligns with your deepest desires.

Day 7:
Reflect on the past week of your meditation journey and how it has influenced your mindset and energy. Notice any shifts in your thoughts, feelings, or behaviors as a result of your practice. Embrace any positive changes you have experienced and use them as fuel to propel you forward. Trust in the process of manifestation and continue to cultivate a strong foundation of motivation and positivity through daily meditation.

Day 8:
Today, focus on aligning your thoughts, feelings, and actions with your desired manifestations. As you meditate, affirm your intentions with clarity and conviction. Repeat empowering statements that resonate with your goals and aspirations. Believe in your ability to create the reality you desire and let that belief guide you in making choices that support your vision. Stay true to yourself and trust that the universe is working in your favor.

Day 9:
With each passing day, your practice of ten-minute positive manifesting motivation meditation becomes more ingrained in your daily routine. Allow yourself to sink deeper into a state of relaxation and focus as you meditate today. Connect with the energy of the universe, feeling its support and guidance surrounding you, know that every moment you spend in meditation brings you closer to aligning with your highest potential.

Day 10:
By now, you have likely experienced the power of consistency and dedication in your daily meditation practice. Take a moment to reflect on how far you have come and how much you have already grown in mindfulness and positivity.

Today, as you sit down for your ten-minute meditation, visualize your goals and dreams with even greater clarity. Envision yourself already living the life you desire, feeling the emotions of success, happiness, and abundance. Let this vision fill you with motivation and excitement for the journey ahead.

With each breath, reaffirm your belief in the power of manifestation and your ability to create the life you envision. Feel a sense of gratitude for all the blessings in your life, and trust that the universe is aligning to bring you even more abundance and joy.

As you conclude today's meditation, carry this sense of empowerment and positivity with you throughout the day. Remember that each day brings you closer to your goals and that with each meditation session, you are strengthening your manifesting abilities.

Day 11:
Congratulations on making it past the halfway mark of your twenty-one-day journey! As you sit down for your ten-minute meditation today, allow yourself to tap into a deep sense of gratitude. Count your blessings and take a moment to appreciate all the good things in your

life, big and small. By shifting your focus to gratitude, you open the doors for even more positivity and abundance to flow into your life. Feel the warmth and joy that gratitude brings, and carry this feeling with you throughout your day.

Day 12:
Today, as you delve into your manifesting meditation, focus on setting clear intentions for what you want to manifest in your life. Visualize your goals and dreams with crystal clarity, as if they are already happening in the present moment. Envision yourself living your best life, feeling fulfilled and aligned with your purpose. Trust in the power of the universe to bring your intentions to fruition and stay open to receiving all the opportunities and blessings that come your way.

Day 13:
Halfway through the second week of your twenty-one-day journey, take a moment to check in with yourself. Notice any shifts in your mindset, emotions, or energy levels since you started this practice. Celebrate any breakthroughs or insights that have emerged during your meditations. If you encounter any challenges or resistance, remind yourself of your inner strength and resilience. Trust that you have the power to overcome any obstacles and continue moving forward on your path toward manifesting your desires.

Day 14:
Today, let go of any limitations or self-doubt that may be hindering your progress. Affirm your worthiness and believe in your ability to manifest your deepest desires. Tap into your inner confidence and courage as you embrace the next phase of your journey. Visualize yourself stepping into a place of unlimited potential and infinite possibilities. With each breath, reaffirm your commitment to manifesting a life filled with abundance, joy, and fulfillment.

Day 15

Today, focus on the changes you would like to see in your life. Visualize how it looks and how it feels living in your new life. Picture the job, the house, the companions you would like to have; soak it up and enjoy the feelings. This is your new life you are embarking on; its your design created by you.

Day 16:

With just a few days left, continue to harness the positive energy and motivation that radiates from within you. As you sit in meditation today, envision the life you desire with clarity and intention. Feel the emotions associated with your manifestations as if they have already come to fruition. Allow this sense of abundance and fulfillment to wash over you.

Day 17:

As you move closer to the end of your twenty-one-day journey, remind yourself of the power of consistency and commitment. Your daily practice has not only strengthened your manifestation abilities but has also deepened your connection to yourself and the universe. Trust in the divine timing of your desires and know that they are on their way to you.

Day 18:

Today, focus on gratitude for the progress you have made and the growth you have experienced during this journey. Take a few moments to express your thanks for the abundance and blessings that surround you. Gratitude is a powerful magnet for more positivity and success in your life. Embrace a mindset of abundance, and watch as the universe continues to align in your favor.

Day 19:
With just a few days remaining, recommit to your practice with renewed vigor and determination. Allow yourself to be fully present in each moment of your meditation, basking in the energy of positivity and manifestation. Visualize yourself stepping into the highest version of yourself, living a life filled with joy, purpose, and abundance.

Day 20:
As you approach the final day of your twenty-one-day manifestation meditation challenge, take a moment to reflect on the transformative journey you have been on. Celebrate the growth, the insights, and the manifestations that have bloomed within you. Trust in the universe and in your own power to manifest the life of your dreams. You are a powerful creator, and the possibilities are endless. Embrace this day with gratitude and anticipation for the beautiful journey that lies ahead.

Day 21:
Congratulations on completing your twenty-one-day journey of ten-minute positive manifesting motivation meditation! Today is a significant milestone in your commitment to self-care and personal growth. Take a few moments to reflect on how this daily practice has enriched your life and brought positivity into your days.

As you sit down for your final meditation session, close your eyes and take a deep breath. Feel a sense of gratitude for the time and effort you have invested in yourself over the past three weeks. Visualize your goals and dreams with clarity, and believe in their manifestation with unwavering faith. Embrace the positive energy you have cultivated within yourself and carry it forward into your future endeavors.

Remember that this twenty-one-day journey was just the beginning. The habits you have established can continue to bring positive changes into your life if you choose to nurture them. Carry the lessons you have learned and the mindset you have developed with you as you move forward, knowing that you have the power to manifest your dreams and create the life you desire.

Thank you for dedicating yourself to this practice. May your days be filled with positivity, motivation, and the belief that you have the power to manifest greatness in all aspects of your life.

Keep shining bright!

Chapter 7

DHARMA

Everyone has their own gift to give others. Natalie Schlute

Dharma is an ancient Sanskrit term with a variety of definitions.

These include "right way of living" (Hinduism), "cosmic laws and order" (Buddhism), and "path of righteousness" (Sikhism).

The common theme through all these definitions is an idea of a certain way of living and being that is aligned with the Grand Plan for humanity.

In the journey of life, there comes a time when we find ourselves pondering our existence, questioning our purpose, and seeking deeper meaning. This quest for understanding often leads us to the concept of dharma, a profound and ancient idea that encapsulates one's true calling, duty, and purpose in life. Discovering your dharma is not just a philosophical exploration but a practical approach to living a fulfilling and meaningful life. In this chapter, we will delve into the significance of understanding your dharma and how it can transform your life for the better.

Dharma refers to the intrinsic nature of all individuals, their unique role in the cosmic order, and the path they are meant to follow in life. Understanding one's dharma involves recognizing one's innate talents, passions, values, and how one can contribute to the world in a meaningful way.

When you align your actions with your dharma, you experience a deep sense of fulfillment and satisfaction. Living in accordance with your true purpose brings a sense of inner peace and harmony.

Knowing your dharma provides clarity about your goals and direction in life. It helps you make decisions that are in alignment with your values and aspirations, guiding you toward a purposeful life path.

Each individual's dharma is interconnected with the well-being of society as a whole. By understanding and fulfilling your unique role, you can have a positive effect on the world around you and contribute to the greater good.

Knowing your dharma gives you the strength and resilience to overcome difficulties and obstacles. It provides a sense of purpose that helps you navigate through tough times with grace and determination.

Exploring your dharma leads to a deeper understanding of yourself, your strengths, your weaknesses, and your true potential. It opens doors to self-discovery and personal growth, enabling you to evolve into the best version of yourself.

Self-Reflection: Take time to introspect and reflect on your passions, your values, your strengths, and what brings you joy and fulfillment.

Seek Guidance: Consult with mentors, spiritual teachers, or counselors who can offer insights and guidance in discovering your dharma.

Experimentation: Be open to trying new experiences, exploring different paths, and stepping out of your comfort zone to uncover aspects of yourself you may not have known before.

Listen to Your Intuition: Pay attention to your inner voice, instincts, and gut feelings. Often, your intuition can guide you toward your true purpose and calling.

Discovering your dharma is a transformative journey that can lead you to a life filled with purpose, fulfillment, and inner peace. By understanding and embracing your unique role in the grand scheme of existence, you not only enrich your own life but also contribute positively to the world around you. Take the time to explore and uncover your dharma, for it is the key to unlocking your true potential and living a life of meaning and significance.

Throughout my two-decade tenure managing a day spa, I stumbled upon my dharma - my ultimate purpose. Delighting in the growth of individuals both personally and professionally, I forged strong bonds with many of the service providers I worked with over the years. Among them, Shawna's transformation stands as one of my most cherished achievements. Enduring tumultuous times marked by her mother's sudden demise, a tumultuous separation from her children's father leading to the loss of custody of her kids, and legal battles over her father's care due to Alzheimer's, we navigated through the principles of the Law of Attr-ACTION and positive behaviors. Years later, Shawna emerged victorious with full custody of her thriving children, a flourishing hair business, and a beautiful home where she cherished memories with her late father. We continue to inspire each other to this day, we are both committed to our personal growth. Her remarkable evolution into a vibrant, positive mother who embraces life with zest and generosity fills me with immense pride.

Following the sale of my day spa, I transitioned into mentoring a select group of close friends and family members in entrepreneurial endeavors within the vending and real estate sectors. This new chapter has revealed the myriad ways of giving back and the profound fulfillment it brings.

A certain way of living and being that is aligned with the Grand Plan for humanity.

Chapter 8
GOALS

If you want to live a happy life, tie it to a goal, not to people or things. -Albert Einstein

During the early 1980s, my dad and I would take walks, and there was a strikingly large modern white house that caught my eye. I would excitedly tell my dad repeatedly that one day I would own a house just like it. I could vividly picture myself inside and imagine the emotions I would feel living in such a place. My dad, puzzled by my fascination because of his lack of appreciation for modern architecture, would question why I would want a house that resembled an office or a hospital. Fast forward to 2013: I turned my childhood dream into reality by constructing a modern masterpiece, a replica of the house I had envisioned for years before. This obviously did not happen overnight, but it did indeed happen!

Bob Proctor, a renowned personal development expert, has formulated a unique approach to setting and achieving goals that has helped countless individuals unlock their highest potential and attain success in various aspects of their lives. Goal setting is a powerful tool that can transform your life, guiding you toward your dreams and aspirations.

Setting Clear Goals:
According to Bob Proctor, the key to successful goal setting lies in the clarity and specificity of your goals. Vague aspirations are unlikely to

materialize into tangible results. To set clear goals, start by envisioning exactly what you want to achieve. Be specific about the outcome you desire and establish a timeline for its accomplishment. Proctor emphasizes the importance of setting goals that are challenging yet attainable, goals that push you out of your comfort zone while still being within the realm of possibility.

Creating a Detailed Plan:
Once you have defined your goals, the next step is to create a detailed plan of action. It's imperative to break down your goals into smaller, manageable tasks that can be accomplished incrementally. By outlining the specific actions you need to take to reach your objectives, you pave the way for steady progress and momentum toward success. (Bob Proctor has many great tips on this)

Visualizing Your Goals:
Visualization is a powerful technique that involves mentally rehearsing the achievement of your goals. By regularly visualizing yourself already living your desired outcome, you program your subconscious mind to work toward manifesting that reality. Please be mindful that it is important to engage all your senses while visualizing, to immerse yourself in the emotions and sensations associated with accomplishing your goals.

Maintaining a Positive Mindset:
A positive mindset is crucial for goal achievement, as your thoughts and beliefs shape your actions and outcomes. By stressing the significance of cultivating a mindset of abundance, possibility, and unwavering faith in your ability to succeed and by replacing limiting beliefs with empowering thoughts, you pave the way for a mindset conducive to reaching your goals.

Taking Consistent Action:
Execution is where the rubber meets the road in goal attainment. Bob Proctor emphasizes the importance of taking consistent, focused

action toward your goals. By staying disciplined, dedicated, and unwavering in your pursuit, you build the momentum needed to propel you toward success. Proctor encourages individuals to embrace challenges as opportunities for growth, viewing setbacks as temporary obstacles on the path to achievement.

In adopting Bob Proctor's approach to goal setting and execution, you equip yourself with a powerful framework for realizing your greatest ambitions. By setting clear goals, creating a detailed plan, visualizing success, maintaining a positive mindset, and taking consistent action, you harness the power within you to transform your dreams into reality. Embrace this transformative process with dedication, determination, and unwavering belief in your potential, and watch as your life unfolds in alignment with your highest aspirations.

Use the early morning to write down your goals and review them. It is also great to text your goals to your accountability partner.

If you don't know what you are striving for, you will certainly not achieve it.

Upon attending beauty school, an unwavering determination surged within me to one day own my own salon. My sister Alisa treated me to a service for my eighteenth birthday at Alan Edwards salon in Beverly Hills. This captivated me with its modern aesthetic, especially the stunning concrete floors. That moment crystallized my vision, and in the early 1990s, I made my salon ownership dream a reality by investing in Tangles. We embarked on a remodeling journey, and it was a natural choice to adorn it with beautiful concrete floors reminiscent of the salon that had inspired me.

Chapter 9

UN-FEAR

Courage is not the absence of fear, but the willingness to act in spite of it.

At the age of thirty, I was married to my first husband, Pete Thorne. Despite our attempts to have a baby, we experienced two heartbreaking miscarriages. The weight of these losses plunged me into a deep depression, causing me to lose my sense of direction. I found myself trapped in a cycle of negative thoughts fueled by fear and anxiety, spiraling downward. It wasn't until I became pregnant with my son, Blake Thorne, that a ray of joy pierced through the darkness. However, even amid this happiness, I found myself drowning in pessimism and worry. Fears of SIDS, autism, and other dangers consumed my thoughts, preventing me from rediscovering the power of the Law of Attr-ACTION.

Fear is a natural human emotion that can either hold us back or catapult us forward in our journey toward living a fulfilling life. Often, it is the fear of the unknown, fear of failure, or fear of judgment that stops us from pursuing our dreams and discovering our true potential. But it's possible to un-fear yourself and cultivate the courage needed to break free from limitations and embrace a life filled with purpose and passion.

The first step toward un-fearing yourself is to acknowledge and understand your fears. Take a moment to reflect on what fears are currently holding you back from living the life of your dreams. Are you afraid of taking risks, making mistakes, or stepping out of your comfort zone? By identifying and acknowledging your fears, you can begin to confront and overcome them.

Embracing vulnerability is a key component of un-fearing yourself, as it allows you to acknowledge your fears without letting them dictate your actions. Understand that it is okay to feel afraid and vulnerable; these emotions are a natural part of the growth process.

To live the life of your dreams, it is essential to set clear intentions and goals that align with your values and aspirations. Take the time to envision the life you desire and break down your goals into manageable steps. By setting intentions and goals, you create a roadmap for yourself that provides direction and purpose.

Courage is not about eliminating fear entirely but about taking bold and inspired action despite your fears. Step out of your comfort zone, challenge yourself, and embrace new opportunities that align with your vision. Remember that growth and transformation occur outside of your comfort zone, and each step you take toward your dreams brings you closer to living a fulfilling life.

Un-fearing yourself and living the life of your dreams is a journey that can be challenging at times. Surround yourself with supportive and empowering individuals who believe in your potential and uplift you on your path. Seek guidance from mentors, coaches, or like-minded individuals who can provide encouragement and perspective as you navigate through your fears. If you suffer from a current or past trauma, it is imperative you seek professional treatment in order to live the amazing life you are seeking.

Un-fearing yourself and finding the courage to live the life of your dreams is a transformative journey that requires self-reflection, vulnerability, and inspired action. By acknowledging your fears, setting intentions, taking bold steps, and seeking support, you can overcome limitations and embrace a life filled with purpose, passion, and fulfillment. Remember that you have the power within you to un-fear yourself and create the life you truly desire.

Chapter 10
CHANGE

Nothing is permanent except change!

When I was thirteen, my parents went through a divorce, which turned my world upside down and stripped away any sense of control I had. The upheaval and unfamiliarity of living between two households left me feeling lost, depressed, and ashamed. Despite my initial resistance to this new reality, after a year of struggling with profound unhappiness, I made a conscious decision to accept and adapt to my changed circumstances. As I began to appreciate the contrast and unique experiences that came with having two separate homes, I found joy in my evolving lifestyle. During this period of adjustment, I started experimenting with drugs and alcohol, I never really enjoyed any drugs, but I did like alcohol, something I would learn to regret later in life.

My choice to embrace change, unexpectedly catalyzed positive results within our family dynamic. My mother, Pat, crossed paths with the man of her dreams, Jim Clark Sr., leading to a fulfilling marriage. Meanwhile, my father rediscovered quality time with me and his extensive family of nineteen siblings in Mississippi. Though I didn't grasp it at the time, this period marked the start of my journey toward embracing change and recognizing its transformative potential. I have not only learned to embrace change, but it also now excites me, and I seek it out, knowing something great is just right around the corner.

Change is an inevitable part of life. It can be intimidating, challenging, and sometimes overwhelming, but it is also the catalyst for growth, transformation, and new opportunities. Instead of fearing change, we should embrace it with open arms and learn to get excited about what the future holds.

Embracing Change

Change often brings uncertainty and discomfort, but it also opens the door to new possibilities. Embracing change means recognizing that the familiar is comfortable, but the unknown is where growth happens. It requires a shift in mindset from resistance to acceptance, from fear to courage.

To embrace change, start by acknowledging your feelings, whether they're feelings of fear, doubt, or anxiety. Understand that it's normal to feel this way when faced with the unknown. Next, reframe your perspective and see change as a chance to learn, evolve, and create a better future for yourself. Embrace the discomfort as a sign of growth and potential.

Getting Excited About the Future

Once you've embraced change, it's time to start getting excited about what's to come. Instead of dwelling on the past or worrying about what might go wrong, focus on the positive aspects of the future. Visualize your bright future filled with new experiences, new opportunities, and personal growth.

To get excited about the future, set goals and create a vision board that represents your dreams and aspirations. Surround yourself with positive influences, whether they're friends, mentors, or resources that inspire you. Stay open to new possibilities and be willing to step out of your comfort zone to explore what the future has in store.

Embracing Change and Getting Excited—A Personal Journey

Remember that change is a journey, not a destination. It's okay to feel uncertain or hesitant at times, but trust in your ability to adapt and thrive. Embrace change as a chance to reinvent yourself, to discover new passions, and to create the life you truly desire.

As you navigate the waters of change, keep your focus on the bright future ahead. Cultivate an attitude of curiosity, positivity, and resilience. Stay open to the lessons that change brings and be willing to grow from them.

In the end, embracing change and getting excited about the future is a mindset shift that requires practice and patience. Trust in your ability to handle whatever comes your way and believe in the endless possibilities that await you. Your bright future is just around the corner, waiting for you to embrace it with enthusiasm and optimism.

People resist *being* changed but can learn to get empowered by positive changes they *choose* to make.

Chapter 11
ACTION

Your doubts create mountains. Your ACTIONS move them- Mel Robbins

In the realm of goal setting and manifestation, the concept of taking action is often an overlooked yet crucial component. Although the laws of attraction emphasizes the power of your thoughts and energy in attracting what you desire, it is only through action that these desires can be materialized. Action is the bridge between your dreams and reality, the missing piece of the puzzle that propels you toward your goals.

Like a magnet needs both poles to attract, the laws of attraction and action work in harmony to bring about the results you seek. It is not enough to simply wish for something or visualize it in your mind; you must also be willing to take tangible steps toward making it a reality. Without action, your intentions remain dormant, unfulfilled potential waiting to be activated.

Taking action requires courage, determination, and a willingness to step outside your comfort zone. It means setting aside fear and doubts and embracing uncertainty with a sense of purpose and conviction. Action is the fuel that propels you forward, the engine that drives your progress toward success.

Whether it's starting a new project, pursuing a passion, or making a significant life change, every action you take brings you one step closer to your goals. It is through consistent, focused action that you turn your aspirations into achievements, your dreams into reality.

Remember, the universe responds to your actions as much as it does to your thoughts and intentions. By aligning your energy with purposeful action, you create a powerful force that sets in motion the manifestation of your desires. So, don't wait for opportunities to come to you; create them through decisive action and watch as your goals unfold before you.

In the journey toward achieving your goals, let action be your constant companion, guiding you toward a future filled with success, fulfillment, and endless possibilities. Take the first step today, and let every action you take bring you closer to the life you envision for yourself. Be careful not to fall into the analysis paralysis trap.

My Action

To live each day with a positive mindset, by setting goals and taking massive action is essential for a better life. By making conscious choices and actively pursuing our goals, I can create a more fulfilling and meaningful existence. Whether it's working towards a healthier lifestyle, cultivating strong relationships, or pursuing our passions and dreams, each step I take towards positivity can have a ripple effect on all aspects of my life. Embracing positivity not only enhances our well-being but also inspires those around us to do the same. Every small action I take towards a positive direction can lead to a brighter and more rewarding future. Practicing taking action will lead to inspired ideas and if acted upon will lead to the desired results and the life of your dreams.

Thank you from the bottom of my heart to all those who have taken the time to read my book on the laws of attr-ACTION. Your support and interest mean the world to me, and I am truly grateful for the opportunity to share my knowledge and insights with you. It is my sincerest hope that the teachings within the pages of my book have inspired you, brought you clarity, and empowered you to manifest the life of your dreams. Your support fuels my passion to continue spreading positivity and light in the world. Thank you for being a part of this incredible journey with me.

Remember you have not failed until you quit! Take massive action and live the life of your dreams!

About the Author

DeeDee Swanson, a native of Bakersfield, California, was born in 1967 to Marlin and Patrica Swanson. She has two sisters, Alisa and Darlene. DeeDee lived in Bakersfield for most of her life until 2022, when she made the bold decision to move to Las Vegas. Despite facing highs and lows in two marriages and divorces, DeeDee found comfort in her son, Blake Swanson-Thorne, who is her world. Along with her beloved pets, two Frenchies and a Chihuahua, DeeDee dedicated 24 years to running Essentiels Spa Et Beaute before starting a successful new venture in real estate in Las Vegas. Embracing 11 key principles transformed her life in ways she never imagined.

Struggling with alcohol and unhealthy relationships, DeeDee discovered the power of the Law of Attr-ACTION. Despite setbacks, she found the clarity and determination to embody the Law of Attr-ACTION, leading her to pursue her dream life in real estate. Her journey reflects resilience, growth, and the transformative impact of positive thinking. DeeDee now leads a fulfilling and empowered life, aiming to inspire others to achieve their own dream lives.

I have never been happier!

www.ingramcontent.com/pod-product-compliance
Lightning Source LLC
LaVergne TN
LVHW012048070526
838201LV00082B/3850